Fat brother
Skinny brother

Copyright © 2019 David Baer
All rights reserved
First Edition

PAGE PUBLISHING, INC.
New York, NY

First originally published by Page Publishing, Inc. 2019

ISBN 978-1-64424-148-6 (Paperback)
ISBN 978-1-64424-146-2 (Digital)

Printed in the United States of America

Fat brother
Skinny brother

David Baer

One brother likes to eat

The other brother likes to stay neat

The skinny brother makes his bed every day

The fat brother says, "No way!"

The skinny brother says to the fat brother, "Stop eating so much, especially chocolates and such."
The fat brother says to the skinny brother, "Please eat more food! It will put you in a better mood!

You don't want to be too skinny for life

You might not get a wife!"

The fat brother wishes he was more neat.

And the skinny brother wishes he ate more meat.

The fat brother says to the skinny brother,

"One day you will gain more weight."

The skinny brother says, "Great!"

If we were both the same

life would be pretty lame!

Actually, our differences are great!

And we are only the age of eight.

The skinny brother says, "One day

we will be all grown up.

The fat brother says, "Yup!"

I love you, brother, even if you are fat.

So the fat brother gives him a friendly pat.

The fat brother says to the skinny brother,

"I love you no matter what!"

"Thanks, brother, I love you too, even

with your enormous gut!"

So they accept their differences,

and they always stay close

because in life that is what matters most!

So, kids, always be kind to your brother.

This will please your mother!

The End

About the Author

Growing up, David Baer's mother used to read him Dr. Seuss books, and he was fascinated with his writing style. That's why David decided to write a rhyming children's story about two brothers. His English teacher in Cocoa Beach High thought that he had a lot of talent for writing. So he has written this book for children and adults to enjoy!